Plant invaders

Souza, D. M

Points: 1.0

Test#: 75025

Lvl: 7.6

Plant Invaders

Plant Invaders

D. M. Souza

Franklin Watts
A Division of Scholastic Inc.
New York • Toronto • London • Auckland • Sydney
Mexico City • New Delhi • Hong Kong
Danbury, Connecticut

Note to readers: Definitions for words in **bold** can be found in the Glossary at the back of this book.

Photographs © 2003: Bruce Coleman Inc./Adrian Davis: 38; Corbis Images: 43 (Raymond Gehman), 46 (Chris Mattison/Frank Lane Picture Agency), 11 (Richard Hamilton Smith); Dembinsky Photo Assoc.: 44, 45 (Dan Dempster), 5 left, 19 (Adam Jones); Division of Forestry and Wildlife, Department of Land and Natural Resources, State of Hawaii: 49; Dwight R. Kuhn Photography: 9; Forestryimages.org: 41 (Charles E. Turner, USDA-ARS); Gary R. Buckingham,USDA-ARS: 30; Jil M. Swearingen: 6 (Naturalist, Cheverly, MD); North Wind Picture Archives: 10, 16; Peter Arnold Inc./Ray Pfortner: 20; Photo Researchers, NY: 21 (E.R. Degginger), 34 (Michael P. Gadomski), 5 right, 26 (Jacques Jangoux), 29, 33 (John Kaprielian), 13, 24 (Jeff Lepore), 40 (William H. Mullins), 32 (William M. Partington), 12 (David M Schleser/Nature's Images Inc.), 35 (Jim Steinberg); Visuals Unlimited: 36 (Derrick Ditchburn), cover, 50, 51 (Mark E. Gibson), 2 (John Sohlden), 14 (S. Strickland/Naturescapes), 23 (William J. Webber).

The photograph opposite the title page shows the troublesome invader crabgrass.

Library of Congress Cataloging-in-Publication Data

Souza, D. M. (Dorothy M.)
    Plant invaders / D.M. Souza.
        p. cm. — (Watts library)
    Summary: Discusses non-native plants, such as the kudzu vine and the tree-of-heaven, which were imported from other countries and now pose a significant threat to the ecosystems of North America.
    ISBN 0-531-12211-5 (lib. bdg.)   0-531-16247-8 (pbk.)
    1. Invasive plants—Juvenile literature. 2. Plant invasions—Juvenile literature. [1. Invasive plants. 2. Plant invasions. 3. Ecology.] I. Title. II. Series.
SB613.5 .S68 2003
581.6—dc21

2002008887

Contents

Some vines grow nonstop, especially where they are unwanted.

Chapter One

The Aliens

If you were born and raised in Texas, New York, Hawaii, or some other state or country, you are considered a native of that place. Plants also have native homes, having grown for thousands of years in a particular region of the world in harmony with other native species around them. However, when some of these plants travel to another region or continent, strange things can happen.

Imagine a vine that climbs so quickly it covers a bike in less than a week and a house in a matter of months. Picture a shrub with bright yellow flowers that spreads across a hillside choking all other vegetation, or masses of floating purplish-blue blooms that prevent boats from navigating. The words *alien*, *nonnative*, or *exotic* are sometimes used to describe such plants that have become invaders. As they spread, they can cause **havoc**.

Some destroy native vegetation and drive away wildlife. Others trigger erosion or increase the chances of wildfires. They affect agriculture, recreation, and natural resources. Billions of dollars have been spent trying to control them, and many people are joining the battle to halt their spread.

The Agents

How do plants travel to other regions or continents and end up where they do not belong? Wind, animals, and water currents often carry their seeds miles from where they normally grow. Much of the vegetation of the Hawaiian and Galapagos Islands sprouted from seeds that drifted on ocean waves. But other plants or their seeds reached new locations with the help of humans or their activities.

During the exploration of the New World in the 15th century, Europeans carried seeds of crops they hoped to grow for food. Stray seeds arrived hidden in fur, feathers, feed, and the bedding of livestock the Europeans brought with them. Later, colonists cut down forests to make room for homes and other buildings. They plowed the land and planted more seeds.

Dandelion and the common plantain were introduced by colonists. So, too, were **medicinals** such as mullein for treating coughs and congestion, and yarrow for healing wounds.

Alien Organisms

Animals, insects, and microorganisms that cause diseases—such as AIDS and West Nile Virus—can also be invaders.

8

Many seeds spread to new places by floating down streams or across oceans.

Colonists often carried seeds from their native lands to plant in the New World.

Seeds of alien bluegrass and white clover turned open spaces into lush lawns and pasturelands.

Ships bringing colonists to the New World often carried stowaway plants and seeds. Before setting sail, the ships' hulls were packed with heavy material to lessen the chance of winds or waves capsizing the vessels. This **ballast**, as it was called, usually consisted of soil, sand, and rocks scooped from coastal waters. Mixed with the debris were the seeds of shoreline plants. At the end of the voyage, when the ballast was emptied, many seeds began growing on new soil.

In 1771, catalogs listing hundreds of exotic agricultural,

ornamental, and medicinal plants became available in the colonies. If a plant did not grow well or was not useful as grain or **forage**, it was discarded. A few throwaways, such as crabgrass, continued growing and spreading.

In the 19th century, the U. S. government actually began a campaign to import what were considered "useful" plants.

Invasive weeds can cost American farmers billions of dollars each year.

Escapees

Benjamin Franklin sent seeds of the Chinese tallow tree, which could be used for candle wax, to a plantation owner in the South. Once established, the tree slowly began growing in nearby wetlands, where its seeds were spread by water as well as by birds. Today, the Chinese tallow has invaded coastal areas from Florida to southern Texas and has wiped out many native grasses.

About 200,000 exotic species were brought into this country, planted in special gardens, and later distributed.

Hitchhikers

Seeds of African rue reached the United States by stowing away on military aircraft and equipment.

During World War I and World War II, the wheels of tanks and aircraft made ideal hiding places for alien seeds. When these military vehicles and other equipment were sent back to their bases, exotics traveled with them. Puncture vine, native to the Sahara desert, entered North America in this way. African rue, another native of the desert, may have reached

Texas and New Mexico on military aircraft. In time, the plants spread to neighboring states.

After World War II, increasing numbers of people traveled to distant countries, saw items they thought were attractive, and brought them back to cities and towns across North America. As demand for foreign goods grew and international trade expanded, food, furniture, lumber, clothing, and household goods were imported and exported. Each item that traveled increased the likelihood of an exotic hitchhiking with it.

Hidden Imports

One traveler, a week after returning from a trip abroad, was surprised to find small alien beetles hatching out of his shirt buttons.

Homegrown Exotics

Not all exotics are from foreign lands. For example, the natural home of the black locust tree is the Appalachian Mountains. Planted elsewhere it was an alien. When allowed to spread, it began threatening the natural environment.

Time Bombs

Not all exotics are troublemakers. For example, irises, tulips, and azaleas have been growing in North America for so long few people realize they are aliens. These plants adapted well to their new environments and grew without competing with native plants. Other exotics, such as oranges, tomatoes, wheat, corn, and oats, became useful in the food industry, and their growth was encouraged. A number of plants, however, were like time bombs. Without the predators and diseases that kept them in check in their places of origin, their populations exploded.

In the 1980s, groups of scientists studying various **ecosystems**, noticed the presence of large numbers of alien plants. They identified more than 4,000 species in the United States

Invaders such as these citrus trees now produce valuable crops.

and Canada, with high concentrations in Hawaii, California, Florida, and the Gulf Coast states. Some of these exotics were having negative impacts. The scientists realized that drastic and immediate actions had to be taken if native ecosystems were to be preserved.

We will now highlight some of these aliens, trace how they arrived, and how they became invasive. Finally, we will show what various organizations and individuals are doing to slow or halt the spread of alien plants before they destroy this nation's ecosystems.

Some Exotics That Pose Ecological Threats

Common Name	Scientific Name	Place of Origin
cheatgrass	*Bromus tectorum*	Eurasia
Japanese honeysuckle	*Lonicera japonica*	Asia
kudzu	*Pueraria montana* var. *lobata*	Japan
leafy spurge	*Euphorbia esula*	Eurasia
multiflora rose	*Rosa multiflora*	Japan, Korea, China
paperbark or punk tree	*Melaleuca quinquenervia*	Australia
purple loosestrife	*Lythrum salicaria*	Eurasia
Scotch broom	*Cytisus scoparius*	British Isles
smooth cordgrass	*Spartina alterniflora*	U.S. Atlantic coast
tree-of-heaven	*Ailanthus altissima*	China
water hyacinth	*Eichhornia crassipes*	South America
yellow star thistle	*Centaurea solsticialis*	Europe

The kudzu plant was first introduced at the Philadelphia Centennial Exposition in 1876.

Chapter Two

Beauty or Beast?

Many animals depend on thousands of native plants for food or shelter. The plants, in turn, rely on the wildlife to pollinate their flowers or spread their seeds. This **biodiversity**, or variety of organisms, is crucial to the health of individual ecosystems.

Some exotics upset this balance in nature. They act slowly, masquerading for a time as things of beauty. But soon their deadly habits betray them.

Unstoppable

In 1876, in celebration of the one hundredth birthday of the United States, countries from around the world were invited to display their goods at the Philadelphia Centennial Exposition. Representatives from Japan created a garden filled with beautiful flowers, trees, and shrubs from their island nation. One plant, the kudzu (*Pueraria montana* var. *lobata*), with large, green leaves and long, purple flowers, especially impressed visitors. Many, eager to plant it in their gardens, carried away slips, seeds, or directions for ordering the vine through catalogs.

Once planted in the southeastern states, kudzu grew in some places as much as 1 foot (30 centimeters) a day. Seeing it as a means of controlling soil erosion, the U.S. government offered to pay farmers to plant the vine. When livestock began eating the leaves, the plant was promoted as a forage crop. Before long, kudzu was growing in gardens, in fields, along roadsides, in vacant lots, and in abandoned yards.

A closer look at the vine reveals how it became so invasive. Kudzu has a **taproot** that often plunges 6 feet (1.8 meters) or more into the ground. Stems spread out in all directions and new shoots sprout every few feet along each stem. After flowers appear in late summer, brown, hairy seedpods develop and the vine quickly multiplies.

Once rooted in southern gardens, kudzu climbed trees and blocked sunlight from reaching leaves. It crawled up telephone poles where the weight of the vine pulled down wires.

Innocent Helpers

During the Great Depression of the 1930s, large numbers of unemployed workers were given jobs through the Civilian Conservation Corps (CCC). One of their tasks was to plant kudzu throughout the South.

It crowded out native plants or completely eliminated them. By 1972 the U.S. Department of Agriculture had declared the plant a pest.

Southerners searched desperately for ways to get rid of it. They dug up small patches, mowed fields, burned them, and applied **herbicides**. Unless the roots were destroyed, kudzu sprouted again. In Japan, the plant was a common ingredient in foods and medicines, so people in this country tried marketing it. They wove vines into baskets, turned blossoms and flowers into jellies and syrups, and leaves into teas. Still, these efforts did little to stop the spread of the plant. Researchers are

In some places kudzu overruns everything in its path.

Backfire

One danger with biological controls is that insects, or other organisms used to stop the spread of invaders, can themselves multiply and cause damage to other plants.

now experimenting with various herbicides and **biological controls**, hoping that one of these can help stop kudzu from conquering the South.

Well-traveled

The tree-of-heaven (*Ailanthus altissima*) is a common sight along fields and forest edges from Maine to Florida and westward to California. It grows next to sidewalks, parking lots, and alleyways in most major cities. People have been admiring and planting the fast-growing **deciduous** tree with beautiful long leaves for over a century without realizing that it is an invader from Asia.

The seed of this tree-of-heaven has grown in an unlikely place.

In 1751, a missionary returning to England from Nanjing, China, brought with him a seedling of the tree-of-heaven. It grew and spread throughout the British Isles and Europe until several decades later colonists carried seeds to Philadelphia. Soon the trees were appearing in nurseries and multiplying throughout the East. Chinese workers coming to California during the gold rush planted seeds around mining sites and helped the tree-of-heaven extend its range in the West.

A mature tree-of-heaven can reach 80 feet (24 m) or more in height. Flowers appear late in spring and are followed by tan to pink fruit. In late summer or early autumn, as many as 325,000 seeds form inside slightly curled papery coverings that fall to the ground or are blown by wind. Eventually, a dense thicket of trees surrounds the pioneer and shades native plants. Toxins in the leaves, bark, and roots prevent other plants from growing nearby.

Once the tree-of-heaven takes over an area, it is difficult to eliminate.

A mature tree-of-heaven produces numerous seeds that are blown on the wind to new sites.

A Celebrity

The tree in the novel *A Tree Grows in Brooklyn,* by Betty Smith, was based on a tree-of-heaven.

21

Cutting only causes numerous suckers to sprout from stumps. Herbicides may kill the aboveground parts, but the roots resprout unless they are sprayed. Two fungi have been found on dead or dying specimens in New York and Virginia, and scientists are hoping that these organisms will become effective biological controls.

Picture Perfect

The multiflora rose (*Rosa multiflora*), native to Japan, Korea, and eastern China, was first brought to this country from Japan in 1866. Nurseries valued it for its small, pinkish-white ornamental flowers but soon recognized that it could have other uses. The tips of its arching stems rooted easily, and with their many sharp thorns the plants made ideal "living fences."

Conservation groups found that the shrubs provided cover for wildlife such as quail, pheasant, bobwhite, and cottontail rabbit. The small bright red fruits, or rose hips, that formed in summer served as food for various birds. Landowners were encouraged to plant the shrubs and sometimes were offered free cuttings. Later the plants were used in highway median strips to serve as crash barriers and headlight dimmers. It did not take long for the multiflora rose to become the invader that it did.

The Japanese honeysuckle (*Lonicera japonica*) was planted on the East Coast as early as 1806. It was used as a ground cover and in the beginning was slow to escape into the wild. Early in the twentieth century, however, it began spreading into nearby areas. Honeysuckle can now be found in fields, along forest edges, and on recently disturbed land as far north as Illinois and Michigan.

The honeysuckle crawls along the ground by sending out numerous runners that produce more runners. It climbs over

Few people realize that these rose shrubs are invaders from Japan.

23

Japanese honeysuckle is a trailing vine that can grow to more than 30 feet (9 m) in length.

shrubs and small trees and soon topples them under its own weight. Aggressive underground roots and buds often interfere with the growth of surrounding trees and plants.

Yellow, tube-shaped flowers appear in late April through July and are followed by small black fruit with seeds that are easily spread by birds. During winter, when many natives are **dormant**, Japanese honeysuckle continues its growth, robbing the soil of nutrients and continuing its conquests of lands. The vine has no natural enemies.

Members of conservation departments in several states have tried repeatedly cutting, mowing, and spraying these two invaders but have had only limited success. The most promising controls to date are biological. Two fungi—one spread by a native mite, the other by a wasp—have been effective against the multiflora rose. Researchers also have introduced whiteflies that are capable of infecting Japanese honeysuckle with a disease.

Water hyacinth has become a troublesome floating aquatic invader in many parts of the world.

Chapter Three

Trouble in the Water

Wetlands and waterways are home to a surprising number of plants that play a vital role in the health of these habitats. Native **riparian** plants create hiding places for many animals. Trees reduce erosion, and decaying leaves, twigs, and stems provide food for fish and other creatures. Riparian vegetation also improves the quality of the water by absorbing excess sediment and pollutants. When invaders take over riparian zones, the ecosystems begin to decline.

Floating Nightmares

The 1885 World's Industrial Cotton Centennial in New Orleans featured exhibits from both southern states and foreign countries. One exhibit from South America displayed water hyacinths (*Eichhornia crassipes*), thick, glossy-leafed plants with showy purplish-blue flowers floating in ponds. Not only did visitors take away slips of the plants to be grown elsewhere, but when the exposition closed, workers dumped the remaining plants into nearby creeks and lakes, where they quickly multiplied.

In the Amazon, home of the water hyacinth, insects, **microbes**, and other competing plants constantly stress the hyacinths and limit their growth. With no predators, the hyacinths reproduce rapidly. In some places their populations double in as few as twelve days.

Water hyacinth's reproductive system is twofold. From the base of the plant short runner stems known as **stolons** radiate to form new offshoots. Stems intertwine and quickly form thick mats that are almost impenetrable. The plants can eventually reach 3 feet (.9 m) in height. The flowers are attractive but signal the presence of a possibly dangerous tangle of growth beneath the surface.

From New Orleans, the water hyacinth invaded the waterways of several southeastern states. By 1895, floating mats were blocking the passage of steamboats and other vessels on several rivers. By 1950, the plants occupied more than 125,000 acres (50,000 hectares) in Florida alone. They were shading

Eating the Problem

In the Philippines, the leaves of the water hyacinth are known as water lilies or *dahon* and are eaten as a vegetable.

and crowding out native plants and affecting fish populations. As dead plants fell to the bottom of lakes and rivers, microorganisms involved in their decay consumed oxygen. Fish died as a result of either the reduced oxygen or the high levels of nutrients from the decaying plants.

The hyacinth reached California and soon spread across that state's lakes and rivers. Chunks of mats broke free and clogged pump stations that supplied water for drinking and irrigation. Mats blocked salmon migrations and made delivery of supplies to island populations almost impossible. Adding to the problem, periods of heavy rainfall triggered the production of many seeds that quickly reached new areas.

Machines are sometimes used to halt the spread of water hyacinth.

Spreading Abroad

Water hyacinths also became a problem in tropical and subtropical parts of Australia, New Zealand, Japan, the Philippines, and Africa.

To control the spread of the plants, workers first used machines to remove them from the water and then ground them into bits. They set up barriers to keep the plants out of navigation channels and sprayed herbicides on them. In 1970, researchers in South America discovered two weevils and a water hyacinth borer that were natural enemies of the plant and helped weaken those growing in the United States. Later, three species of flies collected in Argentina showed promise as biological controls. Researchers are hoping that these tiny jungle enemies will help stop the rampage of this aggressive aquatic invader.

Several kinds of insects are helping to keep water hyacinths under control.

Punk Trees

Big Cypress Swamp, Lake Okeechobee, Everglades National Park, and the Florida Keys are all part of Florida's Everglades—a vast wetland stretching from the center of the state to its southern tip. Since 1950, development has reduced the size of the Everglades by 50 percent and what remains is under attack by a number of exotics. One of the most serious is a tree popularly known as the punk or paperbark tree (*Melaleuca quinquenervia*).

In 1906, John Gifford, a University of Miami professor, was searching for a tree that would grow well in southern Florida. He ordered seeds of the paperbark tree from Australia and planted them in his garden in the Miami area. He also gave away some to a nearby nursery. The tree proved to be a fast grower, reaching more than 50 feet (15 m) in height at maturity. Its whitish bark with many paperlike layers and white flowers made it an attractive addition to the landscape. People began planting it as an ornamental and as a windbreak. Because its roots absorb huge amounts of water, the tree was also recommended for swampy areas.

During their first year, paperbark seedlings grow between 3 and 6.5 feet (1 and 2 m). By the time they are three years old, they are producing small, lightweight seeds, some of which root close to the parent tree. Other seeds float on the surface of the water or are blown by breezes to new areas. Paperbark trees also store massive numbers of seeds in grayish-brown capsules along their stems. A mature tree can

Seeding the Wetlands

In 1936, the owner of a nursery in Miami flew over the Everglades and dropped seeds of the paperbark tree into the wetlands.

Alien punk, or paperbark trees, pose a threat to the Florida Everglades.

release more than 1 million seeds each year and store an additional 20 million.

For almost fifty years, these exotics grew and multiplied in the Everglades until they occupied hundreds of thousands of acres in central and southern Florida. Forests of these trees shaded out native plants, causing them to disappear. In some places, their trunks grew so close together that they formed thickets that even animals could not penetrate.

Efforts to control the spread of paperbark trees have had

mixed results. Some have been cut, but in a short time sprouts grow from stumps. They have been uprooted, but if left on the ground, branches soon turn into individual trunks. Burning or spraying has caused the release of millions of seeds, which in time are able to germinate. Biological controls, such as weevils, sap-feeding sawflies, tube-dwelling moths, and gallflies imported from Australia, have shown the most success. Conquering paperbark trees before they destroy the entire Everglade ecosystem is now the job of these armies of insects.

The Purple Plague

Early in the 19th century a hearty **perennial** was found growing near the port cities of Philadelphia and Boston. The plant, purple loosestrife (*Lythrum salicaria*), was a native of Europe and Asia and had probably arrived in a ship's ballast. Colonists may also have brought it into this country as a medicinal herb for treating wounds and sores.

The plant, with showy pinkish-purple flower spikes, can sometimes tower more than 6 feet (2 m) high. It attracts a variety of bees and other pollinators that are frequently seen

Troublesome Trio

Other exotic trees that are causing the Everglades problems similar to those of paperbark trees are the Brazilian pepper (*Schinus terebinthifolius*) and the Australian pine (*Casuarina equisetifolia*).

33

Purple loosestrife attracts numerous insects and birds that help pollinate its flowers and spread its seeds.

sipping its nectar. Few people suspect that such an attractive plant can become a problem.

After arriving in this country, the colorful plants soon spread all along the New England coast. Capable of producing up to 2.7 million seeds, each as tiny as a grain of sand, purple loosestrife spread to other wetland sites. Some hitched a ride on wildlife or humans and traveled miles away from parent plants. Once they took root, they created thick underwater webs.

With the construction of canals linking rivers to the Great Lakes, purple loosestrife eventually reached Michigan and nearby states. By 1930, it began an explosive invasion of wetlands across all of North America. As of 1996, it was growing in every Canadian province and in every state except Florida.

In the marshes of New England, purple loosestrife has choked out and replaced species of cattails, bulrush, and spikerush. Populations of muskrats and marsh wrens that depend on cattails have declined. As the invader overruns other native plants, more and more animals leave the area.

In North America, purple loosestrife escaped the attacks of a number of insects that besieged it in its native countries. Along with allowing the introduction of aggressive weeds that will squeeze out the loosestrife, importing some of these biological controls seems to be the solution to stopping its spread here. Two species of European leaf beetles, seed weevils, and one root weevil are now meeting that challenge. Many conservationists in both the United States and Canada are hoping that these insect warriors will be able to halt the spread of the "purple plague."

Marshes can quickly be overrun by purple loosestrife.

Scotch broom may be colorful but it is classified as a noxious weed.

Chapter Four

Weeds of the West

Any plant that grows away from its native home can be called a weed. Dandelions are weeds, but they are harmless. Clover is a weed, but it is useful as forage for animals. Other weeds, however, threaten natural areas or agricultural ecosystems. These plants are classified as **noxious weeds**, and they are on everyone's "most wanted" list.

Botanical Bullies

Each spring, western hills, valleys, and roadsides light up with golden-yellow flowers. They bloom on hundreds of shrubs, some of which are 10 feet (4 m) tall. Although beautiful to the casual observer, the shrubs are botanical bullies to those who know them best. Scotch broom (*Cytisus scoparius*) is their name and the British Isles are their place of origin.

In their native habitats, the plants are attacked by twenty-three species of pod- and seed-feeding insects. But in North America, Scotch broom found no predators. It spread across the continent and eventually became one of the most notorious of the western weeds.

Aiding its rapid invasion is the plant's ability to produce abundant seeds. A mature shrub of three to eight years may hold 2,000 to 3,500 brown seedpods, each enclosing up to nine seeds. When ripe, these pods explode, showering their contents in all directions. Birds, small animals, and vehicle tires can carry them miles away. Ants, attracted to oils in the seeds, also help by bringing seeds to their nests.

Scotch broom is not fussy about where it grows. Because the seeds hold their own supply of fertilizer, they grow

Seeds of the Scotch broom hidden inside this pod will soon explode and spread. Some will lay dormant in the ground for up to forty years.

38

A Clean Sweep

The name "broom" is believed to come from the practice of using the long, stiff stems of the plant for sweeping floors.

quickly, and they tolerate drought and cold by sending down deep roots. Disturbed areas, such as newly logged lands, pastures and grasslands, roadsides, and foothills, make ideal growing spots. Once thick stands are established, wildlife is no longer able to forage and moves elsewhere. Young trees, grasses, and native plants also disappear.

Like other invasive exotics, Scotch broom is difficult to eliminate. Cut plants easily resprout. Herbicides require repeated applications. One former enemy of the plant, a seed weevil, has been introduced in several areas. The adult weevil lays its eggs in developing seed pods, and when the eggs hatch, the larvae feed on the seeds. If enough weevils are successful, perhaps the further spread of this yellow bully can be stopped.

Water Hogs

When it first appears each growing season, yellow star thistle (*Centaurea solsticialis*) looks like a poor excuse for a dandelion seedling. In several weeks it bolts toward the Sun, crowding native plants around it and growing up to 6 feet (2 m) tall. While it stretches skyward, it also plunges its roots deep underground and hoards all the water it can find. By the time summer arrives, its blue-green leaves and stems are crowned with bright yellow flowers, each surrounded at its base by

Track Record

Scotch broom now covers millions of acres in California, Oregon, and Washington and threatens endangered oak woodlands in British Columbia.

This bright yellow star thistle flower has sharp spines surrounding its base.

needle-sharp spines in a starlike arrangement. A walk through a field of star thistles is a painful experience.

Star thistle first arrived in the West during the gold rush era. Seeds were hidden in shipments of inexpensive alfalfa from the Mediterranean area, the plant's native range. In the beginning, they sprouted mainly along river edges and gradually spread into irrigated fields. By 1999, these noxious weeds had invaded millions of acres in California, Oregon, Washington, and Idaho.

The fact that star thistle consumes large amounts of water accounts for much of its success as an invader. While the shallow roots of many other **annual** grasses die back and dry out in May, those of star thistle, a perennial, do not. Their deep roots draw up moisture and rob other plants of the life-giving water they need.

Star thistle's abundant seed production assures it a place in the landscape each year. A single plant can release as many as 150,000 seeds. Some of these are able to remain dormant in the soil for up to ten years.

To help reduce the number of star thistles, sheep, goats, and cattle have been encouraged to graze on them. Despite

Horse Trouble

Horses can be poisoned by star thistle. After eating it they may develop "chewing disease," which makes them unable to eat or drink. Sometimes the animals die of starvation and dehydration.

Each star thistle plant has at least 150,000 seeds and can quickly multiply.

Beware!

The scientific name of star thistle, *Centaurea*, comes from the Greek word *Centaur*, which means spearman or piercer.

mowing, burning, and spraying with herbicides, the plants still thrive. The most promising control lies in the use of its natural enemies. Three weevils from the Mediterranean area attack buds, flowers, and seeds. A rust fungus has recently been identified. Its release is awaiting approval so that scientists can be certain that no other plants except the "prickly water hog" will be harmed by it.

The Cheaters

When shipments of wheat arrived in the high sagebrush plains of western North America in the late 1800s, no one spotted the invaders. Hidden in the grain were seeds of downy brome (*Bromus tectorum*), a grass native to Europe and Asia. Soon, everyone was calling the exotic "cheatgrass" because it cheated farmers out of their crops.

Unlike many other grasses, the seeds of cheatgrass **germinate** in fall. Their roots grow quickly, drawing out water and nutrients. By the time winter temperature cools the top layers of soil, the roots of cheatgrass are deep enough to escape frost damage and are able to continue growing. When spring arrives and other grasses are just starting their growth, the invaders have already stolen needed water and nutrients. They flower and produce hundreds of seeds. As dry summer approaches, the parent plant dies back to conserve moisture and its seeds wait for fall rains. Meanwhile, many native seedlings wither and die from lack of water.

Cattle and sheep frequently act as accomplices of cheatgrass. In spring, as the animals eat or uproot many native plants, the invader is not affected. Even if only 2 to 4 inches (5 to 10 cm) of a cheatgrass plant remains, it can still flower

As alien downy brome takes over, it "cheats" farmers out of crops they have planted. That's why it's called cheatgrass.

Seed Spreaders

One study found that during a grazing season a single cow could release as many as 900,000 weed seeds in its droppings.

Fires destroy native plants while allowing the growth of invaders.

and produce seeds. As the livestock move about, they trample the soil and make room for the plant to spread. They further assist by carrying the sharp-tipped seeds to new areas in their fur or feces.

The high flammability of cheatgrass also aids in its spread. In Oregon, for example, land covered with the weed is 500 times more likely to burn than land covered with natives. Lightning, off-road vehicles, target practice—all can trigger fires that ignite cheatgrass and help extend its range. These fires make it difficult for sagebrush and other native grasses to make a comeback. Seeds of cheatgrass not only survive but thrive on the nutrients released by fire. These weeds later produce more seeds than weeds on unburned sites.

Cheatgrass now dominates many sagebrush ecosystems and has invaded forty-eight states as well as the provinces of Canada from New Brunswick to British Columbia. At present, several weapons are being used against it: chemical sprays, reseeding of areas with plants capable of competing with the exotic, and controlled livestock grazing. No biological control has yet been found. It remains to be seen who will win the battle against this weed.

*Horned beetles may help control
the spread of leafy spurge.*

Chapter Five

Counterattack

Fires, tornadoes, hurricanes, and earth-quakes leave devastating trails of destruc-tion. Yet the most costly destructive agents in our nation today are not these natural disasters but exotic invaders. Each year the federal government and state agencies spend billions of dollars attempting to stop the invaders from tak-ing over farms, rangelands, waterways, forests, and national parks. The govern-ment is making progress but cannot do it alone. Thousands of private citizens of all ages have been enlisted to join the fight in different ways.

In the Hawaiian Islands, for example, many people are involved in Operation Miconia, a campaign to root out Hawaii's most threatening plant, a tree that arrived from South America—the miconia (*Miconia calvescens*). The escapee first devastated native plants of Tahiti and is now threatening to do the same in the Hawaiian Islands. Posters of the exotic tree hang from poles around the islands. Public service announcements on television urge everyone to search out the tree. Once the invader is spotted, its location is reported over a hot line. Crews are then dispatched to remove it. Only with this kind of cooperation can the threat be removed from Hawaii.

Each spring and fall groups of volunteers in Washington and Oregon patrol Pacific coast shorelines searching for and eliminating an exotic cordgrass (*Spartina alterniflora*). This plant is a native of the Atlantic coast of North America, but on the Pacific coast it is an invasive alien. It is destroying habitats where clams and oysters burrow and salmon feed. Volunteers, trained to both identify and eliminate this dangerous invader, are helping to reduce its numbers.

In other states, citizens known as weed warriors wage counterattacks against invaders. They learn how to spot plants that are destroying ecosystems. Then they join weed-pulling patrols that scout hills, fields, and national parks searching for the enemies.

Some individuals take a different approach. High school students in Montana, along with their instructor, recently

WANTED:

MICONIA
Dead or Alive

This Miconia tree is 5 feet tall. They can grow up to 50 feet in height.

A Miconia flower stalk contains thousands of seeds.

What is it?

Miconia is a fast-growing, weedy tree from South America that is now invading Hawaii.

- It has large, dark green leaves with purple undersides. Leaves can be up to 3 feet long and are oval-shaped.

- It looks like a bush when young, but can grow up to 50 feet tall.

Why is it a threat?

Miconia shades out other plants in native forests, pastures, and farmlands.

- It causes increased erosion by killing groundcover plants.

- A single plant produces thousands of tiny seeds that spread quickly.

- It has already destroyed 70% of the forest growth on Tahiti.

- Miconia plants have now been found on the Big Island, Maui, Oahu, and Kauai.

What can you do?

- If you think you've found Miconia, call the hotline on your island. An expert will confirm your sighting (several other plants look like Miconia) and will tell you what to do next.

- Share this flier with your family, neighbors, and community groups.

Hotline Numbers:

Big Island 961-3299

Kauai 241-3411
after hrs. 241-3736

Lanai 565-7430

Maui 984-8100
after hrs. 984-8107

Molokai . 553-5236

Oahu 973-9538

Hawaiians are waging a war to stop the spread of the miconia tree, an invasive plant from South America.

Native plants provide ideal habitats for wildlife and make a natural replacement for grass lawns.

obtained 200 horned beetles and reproduced millions more to act as biological controls of leafy spurge (*Euphorbia esula*). The plant, also known as wolf's milk, is a native of Europe and Asia and has invaded prairies, pastures, abandoned fields, and road-

sides across much of the northern United States. The beetles, once released, attack the plants' stems and root system, weakening and eventually killing many.

About 18,000 plants are native to different parts of North America. These plants are attractive, hardy, and do not need watering, fertilizers, or herbicides. They provide food and shelter for insects, birds, and other wildlife. Groups working to eliminate alien invaders are seeding vast areas with a variety of native plants. Some home gardeners are planting native shrubs and flowers in place of water-thirsty lawns.

We cannot completely eliminate every exotic or return the landscape of North America to the way it was before explorers and colonists arrived. We can, however, learn more

Native Plantings Pioneer

Aldo Leopold, author of *A Sand County Almanac* and one of the founders of the Wilderness Society, bought a tract of land in Wisconsin in 1930 and seeded it with native plants.

about plant invaders and discover which ones are growing in and around our neighborhoods. By joining groups and organizations working to control or eliminate the invaders, we can help preserve native plants that provide habitat for thousands of wildlife species.

Glossary

annual—a plant that lasts for only one growing season

ballast—material carried in the hulls of empty or lightly loaded ships to keep the vessels stable in rough waters

biodiversity—the variety of species living in any particular area of the world

biological control—an organism used to stop the spread of weeds

deciduous—shedding leaves each year

dormant—inactive

ecosystem—a community of organisms and the environment in which it lives

forage—food for livestock

germinate—to begin to grow

havoc—wide destruction and confusion

herbicide—a chemical substance used to kill unwanted plants

medicinal—a plant used as medicine

microbe—a microscopic organism

noxious weed—an alien plant invader that has exploded in size and number

perennial—a plant that lives and reproduces during more than one growing season

riparian—situated or growing along the banks of rivers or other bodies of water

stolon—a short horizontal stem that produces new plants

taproot—a deep central root that helps anchor some trees and plants in the ground

To Find
Out More

Books

Collard, Sneed B. *Alien Invaders: The Continuing Threat of Exotic Species.* Danbury, CT: Franklin Watts, 1996.

Guiberson, Brenda Z. *Exotic Species, Invaders in Paradise.* Brookfield, CT: Twenty-First Century Books, 1999.

Lesinski, Jeanne M. *Exotic Invaders.* New York: Walker, 1996.

Patent, Dorothy Hinshaw. *Biodiversity.* New York: Clarion, 1996.

Pringle, Lawrence. *Living Treasure: Saving Earth's Threatened Biodiversity.* New York: Morrow Junior Books, 1991.

Videos and Images Online

The Amazing Story of Kudzu. University of Alabama Center for Public Television and Radio, 1996

Earth Cycles and Ecosystems. Aims Multimedia, 1992.

Plant Life in Action. Library Video Co., 2000.

http://plants.ifas.ufl.edu/
This Center for Aquatic and Invasive Plants at the University of Florida has images of 460 aquatic and invasive plants in Florida and gives ways of identifying them.

http://tncweeds.ucdavis.edu/photos.html
This site features photos of non-native plants that have invaded various areas. Plants are listed by scientific names.

Organizations and Online Sites

American Lands Alliance
726 7th Street, S.E.
Washington, D.C. 20003
http://www.americanlands.org
The goal of this organization is to prevent ecosystems from being invaded by alien species.

Aquatic Ecosystem Restoration Foundation (AERF)

817 Pepperwood Drive

Lansing, MI 48917

http://www.aquatics.org/

This non-profit group conducts research to control exotic plants such as water hyacinth and purple loosestrife.

California Native Plant Society

1722 J Street, Suite 17

Sacramento, CA. 95814

www.cnps.org

This nonprofit organization works to increase understanding of California's native plants and help preserve them.

Center for Aquatic and Invasive Plants

University of Florida

7922 NW 71st Street

Gainsville, FL 32653

http://plants.ifas.ufl.edu

Based at the University of Florida, members study and manage invasive plants and educate the public about them.

The Nature Conservancy

4245 N. Fairfax Drive, Suite 100

Arlington, VA 22203

http://nature.org

The purpose of this organization is to preserve native species and their habitats around the world.

Plant Conservation Alliance
1849 C Street NW, LSB-204
Washington, D.C. 20240
http://www.nps.gov/plants/
This organization is composed of ten agencies of the federal
government working to preserve our nation's native plants.

A Note on Sources

Several summers ago, a hike across a meadow and open hillside near where I live turned into a prickly experience. The land, bright yellow from a distance, was covered with thigh-high plants crowned with yellow thistles that poked and jabbed at my legs. Taking a sample to the nearest office of the Department of Agriculture, I learned that the plants were yellow star-thistles, alien invaders that were causing serious problems in California and several other western states.

Armed with leaflets and information gathered from the department, I began searching the library for books on plant invaders. George Cox's *Alien Species in North America and Hawaii* gave a clear overview of the problem. Two other books, *America's Battle with Non-Native Animals and Plants* by Robert Devine, and *Plant Invaders: The Threat to Natural Systems* by Q. C. B. Cronk and J. L. Fuller, revealed the impact exotics are having on native ecosystems around the world.

Several Internet sites recommended in Cox's book listed additional information and other resources to investigate. Articles in magazines and scientific journals highlighted the efforts being made to stop the spread of alien plants. Not only scientists but also thousands of ordinary citizens are involved in the war against these damaging invaders.

Index

Numbers in *italics* indicate illustrations.

About the Author

Reading about scientific developments and discoveries, exploring forests and seashores, observing wildlife, and introducing young people to the exciting world of nature are some of D. M. Souza's favorite things to do. As a freelancer, she has written more than two dozen science-related books, including *Endangered Plants*, *Freaky Flowers*, *Meat-Eating Plants*, *Wacky Trees*, and *What Is a Fungus?* for Franklin Watts.

DATE DUE			